The Cloud Migration Handbook: Moving Applications and Data to the cloud

ABOUT THE AUTHOR

Srinivasa Rao Thumala is a multi-cloud certified professional with over 20 years of IT experience, specializing in Azure and AWS solutions for Fortune 500 companies. With expertise across Financial Services, Automotive, Telecommunications, and Retail, Srini has successfully led large-scale projects, driving innovation and operational efficiency. At Microsoft, Srini architects infrastructure deployments and enhances cloud solutions, while previous roles at AWS and IBM focused on workload migrations, VDI solutions, and automation. Passionate about technology, Srini shares knowledge through thought leadership and empowers organizations in their cloud transformation journey.

CONTENTS

List of Figures

List of Tables

Chapter 1: Cloud Migration

Cloud Computing

Cloud computing is a new and revolutionary way through which organizations can manage and utilize IT resources. It provides flexible, self-service compute that business can rapidly provision and dynamically scale up and down over the internet.

This means that migrating from operational IT systems to cloud implementations will free organizations from expensive hardware, increase agility, and innovation. In this chapter, the author offers a concise overview of the core characteristics of cloud computing, defines cloud migration, and explores the objectives and challenges associated with the process.

Cloud computing can be described as a model of sourcing where IT resources such as servers, storage, networks or analytics are delivered through internet. For example, unlike traditional practices where organizations had to invest in physical systems, the cloud allows access to these resources on a subscription basis, enabling better cost control.

Major cloud providers like Amazon Web Services (AWS), Microsoft Azure, and Google Cloud have transformed the IT landscape by delivering powerful, secure, and scalable platforms to meet diverse business needs.

One of the biggest advantages of cloud computing is cost savings. There is no need for massive investments in hardware and infrastructure within and between organizations. They can only pay as they use by organizing a system whereby, they are charged according to the amount of resource they require.

It leads to the elimination of resource overprovisioning that is often utilized in traditional centralized environments and offers the ability to scale to the requirements currently present in the business processes. The cloud also provides equal advantage of flexibility where the business can manage its daily workloads with relative ease. For instance, an e-commerce platform used by more customers during a holiday sale can quickly add more resources and not have downtime.

Another advantage of the cloud is in its global accessibility that spurs collaboration and productivity of a team. It helps various employees or teams to access applications and data anywhere, which makes it perfect for workplace decentralization including working from home.

Velocity and versatile also appear to be essential characteristics. Being web-based, solutions can be implemented with relative ease, thus, enabling business faster delivery and creation of new products or services. In addition, cloud platforms have integral disaster-recovery solutions that minimize various perils linked with data loss due to system risks and cyber threats.

Security is still a high-ranking factor for cloud providers who ensure they invest in encryption, compliance certifications and other key access controls. These measures can go beyond what individual organizations can accomplish using their core facilities.

The cloud fosters innovations since it allows one to incorporate new techniques including Artificial intelligence (AI), Machine learning (ML) and even big data analysis. Organizations can apply these tools to amass information, improve organizational decisions, and provide consumers with improved solutions.

Cloud Migration

Cloud migration, simply put, is the process of moving data, applications, rationalizations, and other IT resources from on-premises physical or virtual environments to cloud-based environments. It may also include the process of moving from one service provider to another to suit some specific needs of the business.

Awareness of the cloud's abilities has grown meaningfully, making migration an intentional process instead of a simple IT task. With the help of the cloud solutions, enterprises are able to update their business environments, improve the workflow, and enhance future development plans.

The significance of cloud migration is about customer relevance in a world that is quickly becoming more dependent on the internet. Organizations face growing pressure to remove operational barriers and enhance productivity. These are particular attributes of cloud migration that line organizations up for challenges and help them to leverage an infrastructure that is flexible, cheap, and plentiful to future developments.

The process also helps businesses to avoid the exhaustion and concern of having to manage hardware or software upgrades themselves. For example, moving the company's workloads to the cloud enables that company to refocus its IT personnel's developmental efforts instead of attending to maintenance requirements.

Several factors may motivate modern organizations to pursue cloud migration. One key reason is the potential for enhancing operational efficiency, as cloud platforms automate various IT processes, enabling companies to focus on more critical issues. This efficiency has resulted in greater productivity and faster deployment of applications.

Another compelling strategy is cost reduction since organizations do not require large initial outlay and do not need to pay for the infrastructures. Similarly, it promotes agility and enables organizations to stay up to date with cutting-edge tools and equipment.

The provisioning of more resources during high demand means that businesses are always in a position to adequately prepare itself to cope with growth or with increased workloads. For clarity on the differences between the old systems and the new cloud systems, it's possible to look at the comparison of on-premise infrastructure and cloud infrastructure as shown in table 1.

Table 1 *Difference between On-Premises Infrastructure and Cloud Infrastructure*

Feature	On-Premises Infrastructure	Cloud Infrastructure
Cost Structure	High implementation cost mainly in terms of servers and hardware.	Pay-as-you-go model
Scalability	Limited physical infrastructure	Possibilities to scale are seemingly limitless.
Maintenance	Managed by internal IT teams	Managed by cloud providers
Access	Limited to locations	Available on the world wide web
Security	Security managed in-house	Additional measures put in place by the providers
Disaster Recovery	Complex and expensive arrangements	Managed DR options

Flexibility	Hard to reconfigure quickly	High levels of adaptability while easy to expand.
Deployment Time	Long times for the implementation of new structures	Instant resource allocation
Technology Updates	Manual updates required	The updates occur automatically by the cloud providers
Energy Consumption	Moderately high, with cooling and power demands	Lower, managed by providers
Compliance	Internal teams must work according to the rules set by regulations.	Many times, providers opt for some form of compliance certification
Upfront Investment	There are considerable costs for vehicles, setup, and licenses also with this solution.	Minimal initial cost
Performance	Limited by existing resources	Capable of offering high performance to demands.

Adopting cloud solutions is a significant step toward achieving cloud-based operations for businesses as they aim to transform and expand in an increasingly digital world. As the subsequent chapters will detail it, cloud migration is a plan, which is implemented, managed, and managed within an organization. For benefits of Cloud Migration see Figure 1 below.

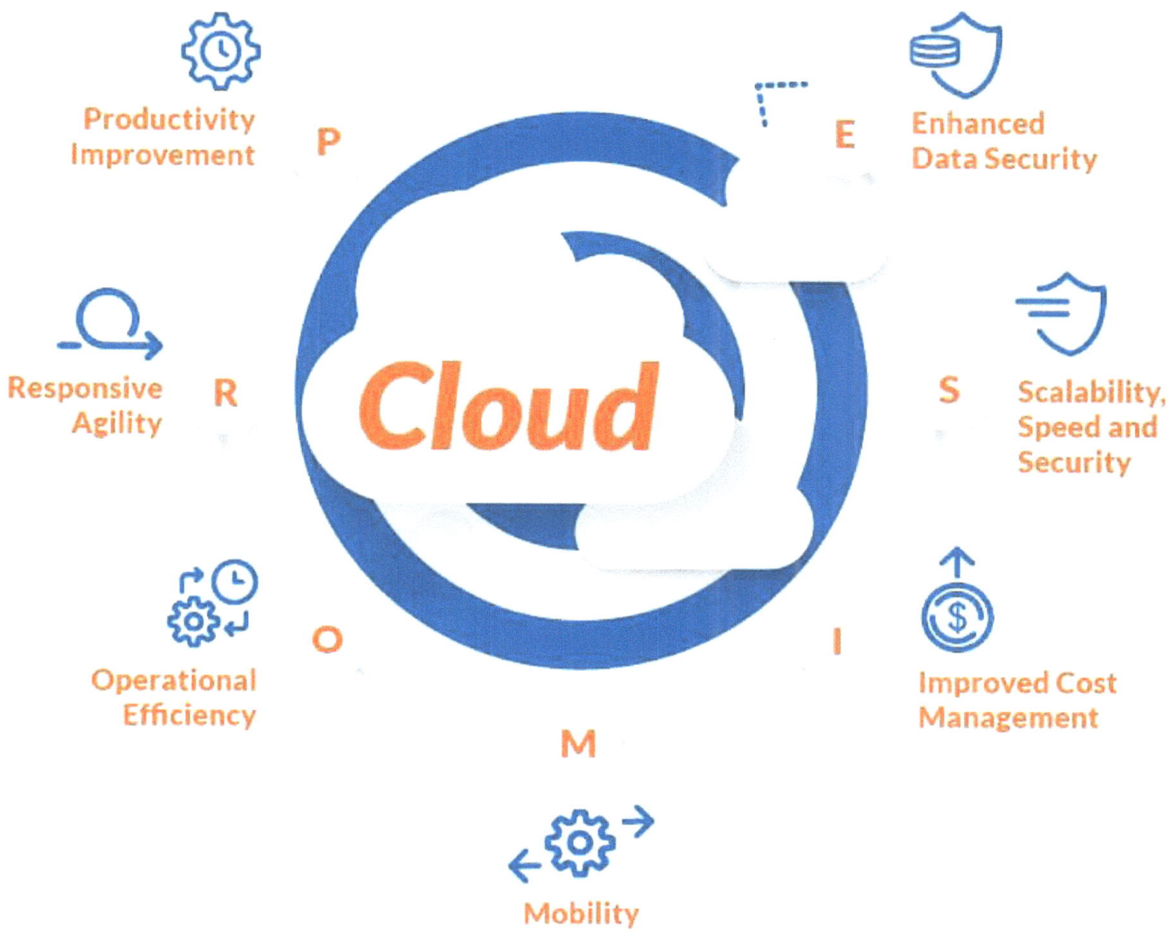

Figure 1 Benefits of Cloud Migration

By identifying the positive aspects, difficulties, risks and purposes tied to the cloud business, companies can successfully get on a cloud route that will lead them to sustainable and stability in uncertainty of continuously progressive technologies.

Challenges and Motivations

It is evident that cloud migration has several advantages, but organizations face numerous difficulties on their way.

- Before migrating, issues related to data security and privacy come into play which are crucial specifically with things such as GDPR or HIPAA.
- Negatively implemented migration can affect continuity of business and may cause loss of potential revenue and low customer satisfaction.

- Old systems can also pose certain compatibility issues with contemporary cloud platforms that may make migration process slightly an issue.
- While cloud adoption offers cost savings, unused or inefficient workloads can lead to additional expenses.
- Moving to the cloud involves staff with great understanding of cloud infrastructural design and management which few organizations have put in place.

However, the reasons to migrate are normally more appealing than these challenges noticed above. Companies seek reach, reduced cost, increased output, and new technologies. By following the above and addressing all the challenges experienced, an organization will be guaranteed a positive experience with cloud migration.

Chapter 2: Cloud Migration Strategies

Cloud migration is not an easy process, but it must be accomplished in steps according to the type of business involved. There are six strategies which are widely considered to attain the successful migration results.

Rehost, Re-platform, Repurchase, Refactor, Retire and Retain. What matters is that those strategies provide different approaches to how workloads should be moved to the cloud to fit the company's needs and technical capabilities.

Rehosting

Lift and Shift also known as rehosting refers to the process of migrating applications and data into the cloud with minimal or with no requirement for changes to the original design. This can lead to immediate cost savings, enhanced scalability, and improved infrastructure performance, all while minimizing disruption to ongoing operations.

Companies prefer rehosting when the need arises to reduce their working time or increase capacity. For instance, a retail business aiming to handle increased traffic during festive seasons might rehost its e-commerce website on cloud platforms like AWS or Azure.

It is a plus for the organisation to be able to leverage on cloud scalability while still having the application standard. However, the primary drawback of rehosting is its inability to fully leverage cloud-native capabilities, which can result in higher operational costs or reduced performance.

Re-platforming

Re-platforming means making slight changes to applications during migration to the cloud to make them better suited to run in the cloud. It means that through re-platforming, businesses are allowed to leverage specific attributes of cloud while maintaining the overall structure of the applications.

For instance, a company could move databases to managed services – like Azure SQL Database or Amazon RDS. It reduces the workload for IT teams in managing databases, allowing them to focus on more critical tasks.

This strategy is usually preferred because of its relatively low cost in terms of human and financial resources and the operational efficiency it delivers which is so necessary for today's organizations, which do not want to redesign the company again but need an improvement.

Repurchasing

Repurchasing means that organizations replace aging systems with systems designed from the ground up to use cloud computing, for example, software as a service. Businesses using this strategy usually want to eliminate redundancies and gain higher functionality provided by SaaS solutions.

An example of this is when a business decides to move from a traditional CRM setup that requires the company's servers to hosting it through the cloud, to using an online service like Salesforce. Repurchase, means that there is no need in maintaining the infrastructure, but at the same time it offers users real top-shelf functionality. However, it means implementation of new systems, which usually comes with new costs of licensing, training, or even customization.

Refactoring

Re-factoring means changing the applications that must be based on the cloud native features. The above strategy is especially suitable for the organizations that are seeking sustainable growth, affordable value delivery and creativity.

Refactoring provides organizations with an opportunity to decompose large-scale applications into microservices, use serverless solutions, or integrate containerization. For instance, a fintech firm could implement a refactoring process to change the payment processing application into microservices with the intention of embracing agility and frequent update.

This is a very effective approach for many reasons, though it can be highly time-consuming, and requires a lot of effort and quite a lot of specialist knowledge. Due to the availability of various strategies, it means that for the implementation of these models, appropriate resources and time must be allocated in the right manner.

Retiring

Retiring applications includes finding and planning the non-usage of a particular system that is not needed any more or is outdated or non-conforming to organizational goals. This strategy has the benefit of making organizations more efficient by decreasing cost, rationalizing their IT networks and freeing up resources previously engaged in managing IT.

For instance, when an organization is undertaking a cloud migration process, it can opt to dispose of old reporting applications that have been supplemented with better analytical applications. In doing so, they avoid creating technical debts that may clutter the organization and provide space for relevant projects.

Retaining

Workload retention entails the maintenance of some applications in their original environment either due to legal, technological, or cost restrictions. It is used for the systems that cannot be migrated without potential risks, but the strategy can also be utilized for critical systems.

For instance, a particular healthcare platform will decide that patient records are best stored and managed within the provider's facilities due to legal requirements to protect the information contained in these records. Keeping those important workloads in focus would help maintain stability while the organisation can start considering migration to cloud for other systems systematically.

It should be noted that any of these migration strategies has its strengths and weaknesses. Essentially, table 2 is aimed at comparing the strategies based on the table with the reference to their put into operation.

***Table 2** Comparison of Cloud Migration Strategies*

Strategy	**Pros**	**Cons**	**Use Case Example**
Rehost	Fast. Minimal changes required.	Some flexibility might be lost and there may well be opportunities for wasted effort.	Relocating a website during the relatively low traffic season to accommodate more customer traffic in other seasons.
Re-platform	Enables minor optimizations.	Has several options that need some alteration, and which	Copying all the data from a local system to a cloud managed system.

	Improves performance.	should be implemented by experts.	
Repurchase	Simplifies management. Access to advanced features.	Licensing and training costs. Limited customization.	The transition from an old-fashioned CRM system to one within the cloud like Salesforce.
Refactor	Maximizes cloud benefits.	Resource-intensive. Implies large time and efforts consuming.	Transforming an existing centralized monolithic application into a microservices architecture to enhance agility.
Retire	Reduces costs. Simplifies the type of workload deployed on IT.	Portfolio needs to be assessed with great attention.	Solving a problem of decommissioning unused applications.
Retain	Reduces interruptions that are unrelated to lesson content and times. Ensures compliance.	Reduces the positive impact of cloud services.	To maintain patient records legal and compliance, patient records system should be managed by on-premise.

Choosing the migration strategy is always considered a strategic decision since it depends on the application type, business needs, available resources and the existing legal requirements. It is therefore possible to use a structured decision-making process supported by decision tree flow chart to identify which approach best suits the various workload of an organization. See Figure 2.

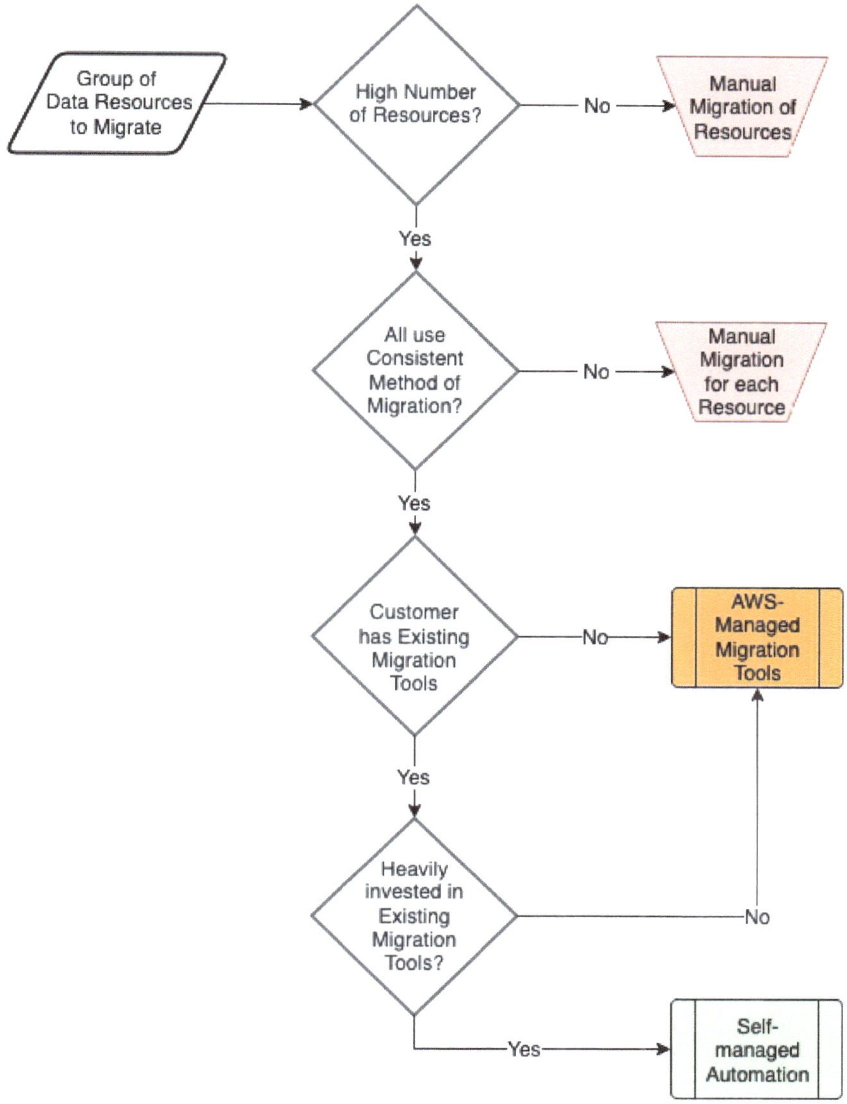

Figure 2 *Decision Tree Flowchart*

The essence of these six approaches is that organizations invariably use one or a combination of them as the solution to different demands of applications. For instance, a manufacturing can rehost their supply chain management system, refactor their inventory tracking application and retire their older order processing software.

This way businesses can manage the issues that prevent effective cloud adoption and unleash benefits that cloud environment provides. It is not a set and forget model; as organizations progress through the lifecycle of cloud adoption they can build, evolve and optimize their migration strategies.

Chapter 3: Cloud Adoption Framework

The Cloud Adoption Framework (CAF) is a comprehensive strategic roadmap that provides organizations with all the essential information needed for successful cloud migration. CAF was devised by the cloud service providers, which provide specific frameworks to elaborate coherent and hierarchical structures to cope with quite challenging issues connected with cloud implementation and the corresponding risks.

They enable an organization to find a way on how to transform and become a cloud organization that works in harmony with the organizational goals and objectives. CAF outlines core reference points that include strategy, readiness, governance, platform, security, and operation, which when implemented can lead to a good cloud transformation.

Pillars

The CAF is made up of six main domains, all of which stand for fundamental aspects that any organization should reflect upon when using the cloud. See Figure 3.

1. Strategy: The strategy pillar deals with the need to link cloud use with organizational goals and the cloud management model. It suggests defining the aims, objectives or purposes of the organization of interest based on areas of interest, for instance; cost, speed, size or value.

   From the achievement of clear goals, it will be easier to determine the strategic workloads and the utilization of resources. This pillar also includes the creation of a financing strategy as well as presentation of the necessary business case that will endorse cloud adoption by multiple stakeholders.

2. Readiness: Training tests an organization's responsiveness to the cloud computing approach which is a broader term than technical compatibility that includes technical, cultural and skills aspects. It entails the assessment of the current state of all IT infrastructures, applications and workforce.

   There is a need to enhance skills and train people who run and manage teams that tend with cloud environments. Readiness also entails creating cloud landing zones which refers to a factory installed infrastructure that is used to host the workloads.

3. Governance: The governance pillar makes sure that the cloud is deployed something that meets proper standards. It covers control for costs and expenses, resources and compliance.

Governing norms provide role and responsibility descriptions for cloud activities, promoting responsibility and lowering risk levels. The last is crucial for industries with specific legal standards for businesses in health or finance.

4. Platform: The platform pillar encompasses the technology infrastructure needed for the cloud workloads accomplishment. It is about creating highly available and flexible solutions based on cloud services.

This pillar also refers to the incorporation of instruments for automation, monitoring and management in the operations. An effective platform management allows organizations to harness the benefits of cloud while at the same time keeping the performance and reliability of an organization's systems into consideration.

5. Security: The CAF has made security one of the foundational domains, which include data protection, user identity, and threat detection. It measures the provisions of sound security policies, secure means of encrypting data and right measures of access.

Security frameworks also include the identification of measures to take during a breach, as well as a phase in which to restore systems in case of a breach. The cloud always provides security tools, including artificial intelligence that helps an organization to strengthen its protection mechanisms.

6. Operations: The operations pillar deals with workload management and another related aspect of cloud manufacturing use. They include assessment of performance, checking for availability, and often auditing.

This pillar focuses on maintaining new and improved ways of doing things to unlock the highest value of cloud expenditure. Various client backup, restoration and scalability processes are also commonly done automatically.

Figure 3 *Six Pillars of CAF*

Mitigating Risks

Reducing the risk associated with migration is one of the central goals of the CAF. The framework also supplies several methods that can be taken to avoid these issues or face them in a better manner where a transition is inevitable.

The first is assessment of the current environment. That is, assessing infrastructure, determining important workloads, and defining interdependencies. It is also useful when there is an inventory of what applications currently exist, so the organization knows how big or small migration is and what tasks need to be done next.

The migration strategy which is formulated next must incorporate the CAF pillars. With the help of the strategy pillar, organizations can define goals and indicate deliverables or known as KPIs. This step also contains all the financial data of estimating costs and evaluating possible savings.

Once a strategy is developed, then readiness activities become visible. Businesses must ensure they are equipped, by having programs that train the teams, upgrading them, or certifying them.

Creation of cloud landing zone is authorized in this phase of the planning process.

The various governance frameworks are adopted next to adhere to compliance and accountability issues. This comprises of policies regarding resources, expenses, and protection of data in the intended business.

Tagging mechanisms are mostly employed in organizations to help monitor resources in the cloud for identification and billing purposes. Agreement also involves setting up of escalation procedures in case of resolving a certain problem or dispute.

The platform pillar is engaged during the architecture and design stage of the program. Some organizations use native cloud services for constructing effective and secure environments. Some of the activities include provisioning and configuration of resources, and scaling made easier by the automation tools hence eliminating the chances of making mistakes. See Table 3 for the checklist.

***Table 3** Checklist*

Element	**Strategy**	**Readiness**	**Governance**	**Platform**	**Security**	**Ops**
Define objectives	☑					
Identify KPIs	☑					
Assess infrastructure		☑				
App dependency mapping		☑				
Train workforce		☑				
Cost management policies			☑			
Define roles			☑			
Scalable architecture				☑		
Automation tools				☑		☑
Identity & access (IAM)					☑	

Data encryption					☑	
Vulnerability tests					☑	
Monitoring systems						☑
Backup automation						☑
Compliance monitoring			☑			

Security features are built-in into the migration process, wherever possible. IAM today compels only the eligible employees and personnel to gain access to the important data. Data encryption ensures that data is secured when it is in movement and when it is preserving. Frequency assessments and security tests define possible threats, and organizations can prevent them.

The last of the advocated key areas is operations to enable smooth workflow of the workload. The tools for performance monitoring are continuously assessing value and time metrics, such as latency and resource load.

This specific solution comprises of backup and disaster recovery in its automated condition as a safety measure for the system. In addition, organizations perform periodic checks, known as audits, to determine optimizations to increases operating efficiency and decrease costs.

Organizations adopting the CAF obtain a disciplined and integral framework for migrating to the cloud. As a result, through considering six basic principles, it is possible to manage migration properly and reduce potential risks for enterprise.

The CAF also guarantees technical and operational coherence for practices and serves as a mechanism for aligning practices with extreme organizational objectives. Run fractional tests, inspections, and modifications of governance and safety procedures support the proper correspondence to the changing business requirements and the progress of IT. Incorporating the Cloud Adoption Framework (CAF) into an organization's cloud adoption processes enhances the effectiveness of cloud utilization while fostering its forward-looking capabilities.

Chapter 4: Landing Zone Deployment

Landing zone is the fundamental model that underpins all cloud migration initiatives. Landing zone is a concept of an initial environment that is secure and designed based on scale for hosting the workloads.

There is confidence that migrated applications and data are correctly placed into a more structured architecture with all the policies, networking and identification requirements put in place as a result. Setting up a landing zone is not just technical in nature, but it remains a fundamental of operations in cloud computing.

Landing Zone

Landing zone can be defined as a roadmap of the organization's workload placement in the cloud. It allows to include critical components such as governance, compliance, networking, and identity management into the coherent concept and implement them in the framework of the unified architecture. It enables a business to promote conformity with the different cloud settings, minimize configuration mistakes, and achieve the most excellent cloud procedures right from the start.

The primary importance of landing zones stems from their critical role in maintaining security and compliance. Organizations that are transitioning to the cloud, they experience challenges like different security policies and incorrect resource configurations. These risks are avoided by ensuring that a structured landing zone forms the basis for safe policy-based cloud operations.

For diagram, see figure 4.

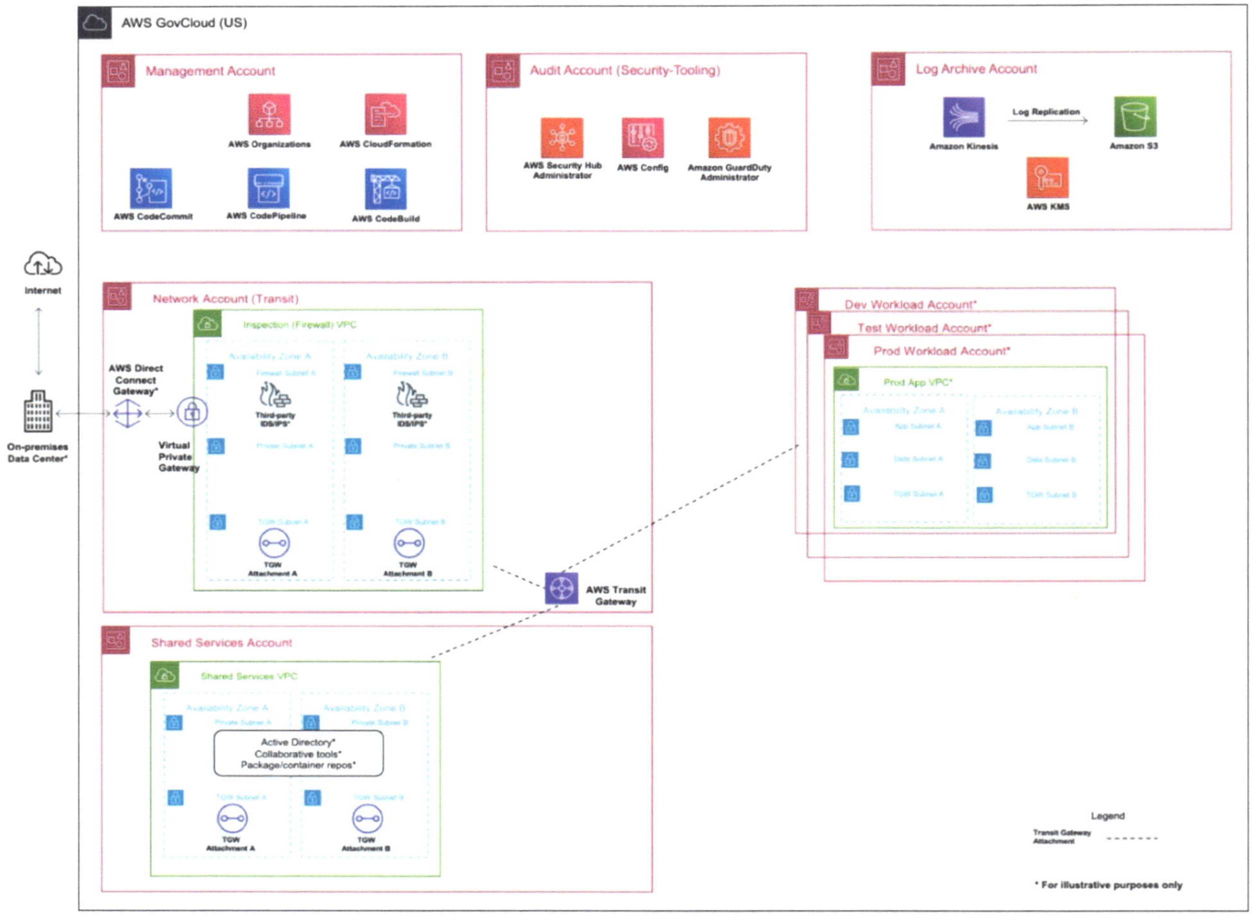

Figure 4 *Architecture Diagram for Landing Zone*

The diagram illustrates the inclusion of the networking layer, security controls, and identity management integration as components of the landing zone.

Landing Zone for Migration

Migrating applications and data to the cloud without a landing zone is like constructing a home without a strong foundation. Extension to the landing zone also makes sure that workloads are set correctly with networking configurations, permission, and monitoring systems in place.

For example, suppose an organization moving its database to the cloud. Without a suitable landing zone, the database could get placed in an environment having less than optimal security measures or perhaps no good identity solutions, thus exposing the database to the risk of compromise. The use of a landing zone helps avoid such questions as it prescribes how identical resources must be managed and deployed.

The landing zone will support the growth of organization's cloud environment. With an increasing number of companies utilizing the cloud, the landing zone again offers the framework for adding resources as the business grows, without having to re-architect the foundation constantly.

Key Considerations

There are several significant factors to consider when deploying a landing zone:

- Networking: Network configurations represent one of the foundational components of implementing a cloud environment. Landing zone should be including virtual networks, subnets and routing tables to facilitate the communication of the cloud resources. Also, NSGs and firewalls should also be put in place to avoid the process of unauthorized access.
- Identity Management: Security of an organization's resources is another major concern in cloud computing and identity management is important for facilitating control on cloud resources. Azure Entra ID or AWS IAM must be integrated as identity providers to enable role-based access control and multi-factor authentication.
- Security Policies: A landing zone needs to have compliance with encryption, establish standards for logging and monitoring, and data loss prevention controls. Thus, by integrating these policies into the organization's landing zone people will automatically follow them.

Steps

1. Start with business and technical assessment of the organization. Identify your high priority workloads, regulations, and objectives for growth.

2. Select one out of the several frameworks that are offered by the cloud provider as its landing zone. For instance, AWS Control Tower, Azure Landing Zones accelerator or Google Cloud Deployment Manager supply pre-configured patterns for the creation of landing zones.

3. Construct virtual networks, subsets of those networks, and routing of those networks. Services that should be added for security are NSGs and firewalls.

1. Define identity providers and maintain the use of RBAC policies. This is where the usage of MFA for all privileged accounts should be enabled.

2. Understand what encryption must be applied, deploy the relevant means of control, and specify the means of logging. Remote operation to permit alerts for suspicious activities.

3. Staging environment to stage deployment of the landing zone. Check the configurations with compliance standards and security standards that needs to be met.

4. After that, deploy the landing zone to production environment or, in other words, roll it out. Workloads should be added to the supplier while configurations are to be constantly monitored and updated.

Terraform Script

The following Terraform script, serves as a basic blueprint to execute a landing zone onto AWS. It is designed to create a VPC, subnets and an IAM role which only has a few privileges.

See Figure 5 for the following code snippet.

```
provider "aws" {
  region = "us-east-1"
}

resource "aws_vpc" "main" {
  cidr_block = "10.0.0.0/16"
  enable_dns_support = true
  enable_dns_hostnames = true
  tags = {
    Name = "MainLandingZoneVPC"
  }
}

resource "aws_subnet" "subnet_a" {
  vpc_id     = aws_vpc.main.id
  cidr_block = "10.0.1.0/24"
  tags = {
    Name = "SubnetA"
  }
}

resource "aws_iam_role" "landing_zone_role" {
  name               = "LandingZoneRole"
  assume_role_policy = <<EOF
  {
    "Version": "2012-10-17",
    "Statement": [
      {
        "Effect": "Allow",
        "Principal": {
          "Service": "ec2.amazonaws.com"
        },
        "Action": "sts:AssumeRole"
      }
    ]
  }
EOF
  tags = {
    Name = "LandingZoneIAMRole"
  }
}
```

Figure 5 *Terraform script code snippet*

This script brings up a VPC and a subnet and also creates an IAM role for purposes of access control. It can be further expanded to other groups such as security groups, logs configurations and monitoring tools.

Creating a landing zone is one of the key migration stages that define the subsequent functioning of a cloud environment. Thus, recognizing significant aspects like networking, identity, and protection it is possible to build a suitable context for business strategies and organizational goals following legal requirements and organizational performance measures.

Landing zone can be defined as the primary foundation of businesses that tend to adopt cloud computing as soon as possible and, therefore, must be effective in order to help companies leverage the benefits derived from actions made in this domain.

Chapter 5: Cloud Service Models

Cloud service models serve as the basis of today's business activity, while differing by the degree of abstraction and manageability. Out of those three models, there is Infrastructure as a Service (IaaS), Platform as a Service (PaaS), and Software as a Service (SaaS). One is designed for greater control but lesser convenience while the other offers convenience with moderate control and better functionality, which makes a necessity for acquisitions in various industries.

Cloud Service Models

- **Infrastructure as a Service (IaaS)** can be defined as the provision of fundamental computing resources such as server usage, storage space and network components, where the consumer is billed based on usage. It brings users the greatest control of their environment since the systems – be it the operating systems, applications, and configurations. As mentioned above IaaS is more suitable for organizations planning to adopt scalable services with the flexibility of controlling resources without handling physical hardware. These are for example Amazon EC2, Google Compute Engine or Microsoft Azure Virtual Machines.
- **Platform as a Service (PaaS)** commonly offers infrastructure management as an abstract and delivers a platform for the application. Because it is a manged service, there are no servers or OS platforms to administer; consequently, testers can concentrate exclusively on scripting and advancement. Some of the examples of PaaS are Azure App Service, Google App Engine and AWS Elastic Beanstalk.

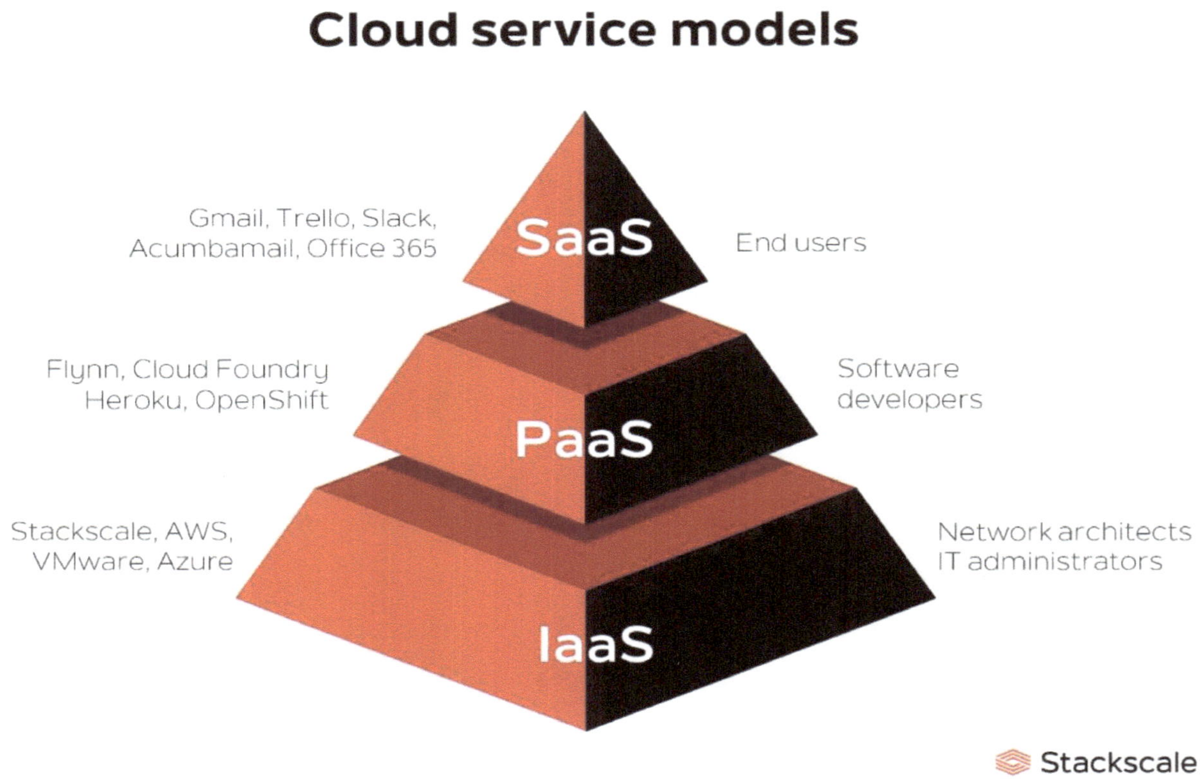

Figure 6 *Cloud Service Model*

- **Software as a Service (SaaS)** refers to the practice of running fully functional applications and software over the internet. It is based on web application, so no installation and no need for maintenance on the users' side. They include Google Workspace, Salesforce CRM, and Microsoft 365 respectively. SaaS is user-friendly and easily scalable hence popular to use among individuals who are not very conversant with technology.

Using the models is different but each offers unique benefits depending on the application involved. IaaS is better if an organization wishes to have total flexibility over the environments that it deploys while PaaS is more appropriate if an organisation needs to create many applications rapidly. SaaS is most suitable for users who require application software which is already operational as soon as they commence its use.

The main differences refer to the degree of abstraction and the roles delegated and played by the user and the cloud provider. With IaaS, all of the management occurs above the operating system level, and with PaaS, even infrastructure and runtime are handled by the provider.

Which means that in SaaS customers can simply use the software with most of the work handled by the provider.

Trade-offs

While use of each model has its positive side, it has its drawbacks too.

- IaaS has its advantages, and the disadvantage is that it is highly technical. Consumers must provide the adequate security, scalability as well as performance.
- PaaS provides a convenient application designing platform and development yet, it tends to bind users to the specific platform thus drawbacks of portability.
- SaaS is incredibly flexible but provides the lowest level of customization, which can cause issues in companies needing more customization or dealing with sensitive information.

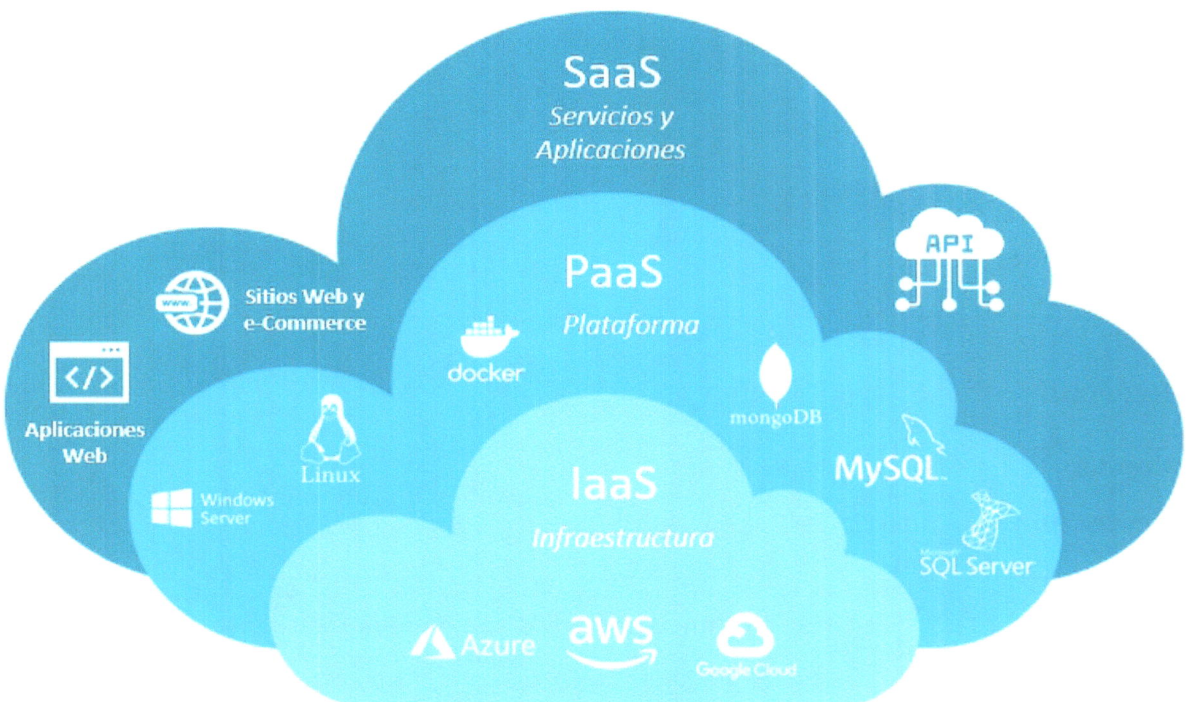

***Figure** 7 Cloud Service Models*

Examples

There are plenty of options for IaaS, PaaS, SaaS services, while leaders of this market are Amazon AWS, Microsoft Azure, Google Cloud, which offer specific options for clients. For instance:

- IaaS: Amazon EC2, Azure Virtual Machines are quite popular for customization needs of applications that require a lot of specific settings.
- PaaS: Azure App Service enables people to build and host web applications on the cloud platform without bothering about the infrastructure to be used.
- SaaS: It delivers CRM solutions to varied businesses without size barriers, with the flexibility of its solutions.

Comparison

A comparison of IaaS PaaS and SaaS is presented in the table below highlighting the features, business use, and examples of each Table 4.

Table 4 *IaaS, PaaS and SaaS Comparison*

Feature/Aspect	**IaaS**	**PaaS**	**SaaS**
Control Level	High	Medium	Low
User Responsibility	OS, runtime, applications	Applications	Usage only
Provider Responsibility	Hardware, networking	Hardware, OS, runtime	Everything
Use Case	Hosting custom apps	Rapid development	End-user applications
Scalability	Flexible	Automatic	Predefined
Setup Time	Moderate	Quick	Instant
Examples	AWS EC2, Azure Virtual Machines	Azure App Service, Google App Engine.	Salesforce, Google Workspace

Customizability	Extensive	Moderate	Limited
Dependency	Requires technical expertise	Platform lock-in risks	Minimal dependency
Flexibility	Maximum	Moderate	Limited
Security Control	User-defined	Shared	Provider-defined

This table shows the ways in which these models diverge in relation to the functions they serve, the people with whom they engage, and the degree of oversight provided by the management. The advantages and disadvantages of both flexibility and simplicity are seen and organizations get to choose the kind of model that they would want to go for.

Benefits

The decision made on the type of service model defines the effectiveness, cost and feasibility of the service model. With IaaS the environments are constructed in a way that makes them optimal for use by the organizations. PaaS speeds up development as it leaves behind infrastructural concerns only allowing the developers to concentrate on the apps. SaaS provides unprecedented convenience since it provides businesses with ready-made tools without having to undergo set-up.

For instance, a startup can first use SaaS to satisfactorily acquire collaboration apps, but later use IaaS as it scales to host a homegrown application. This kind of flexibility helps organizations to modify their approaches over time while trying to overcome all barriers related to both models.

IaaS, PaaS and SaaS are the foundational models of cloud services that help organizations to enhance digital transformation solutions for their multiple requirements. All these models have different pros and cons as well as different levels of control that give them different uses.

These models are essential for understanding how businesses organize the operational and strategic environment while planning for their needs. So, when used in combination, IaaS, PaaS, and SaaS can be truly effective to enhance efficiency and make organizational change

on the way to the cloud.

Chapter 6: Migrating Workloads

Moving workloads to the cloud is a critical step in the process of cloud migration and is considered by many to be one of the most critical steps in a migration process. The challenge is to accomplish these goals as smoothly as possible, while being able to transition data values, interrupt the business processes to minimal extent, and meet the needs of compliance.

Migration has however been characterized to require a good strategizing, proper tools, and understanding of different workloads and data that are involved. This section discusses challenges of moving servers, managing both the unstructured and structured type data and the tools used in migration.

Migrating Servers

Server migration is an important part of the migration process which involves moving VMs and physical servers. Different kinds of a server pose different problems and call for different strategies.

Migrating Virtual Machines

Virtual machines are widely used in modern IT infrastructure because they offer flexibility and software implementation independence. Migrating VMs to the cloud is usually seen as fairly basic, particularly when using Azure Migrate, AWS Application Migration Service and Migrate for Compute from Google Cloud. These tools facilitate critical tasks, and they include identification of dependencies, compatibility analysis and deployment of configurations.

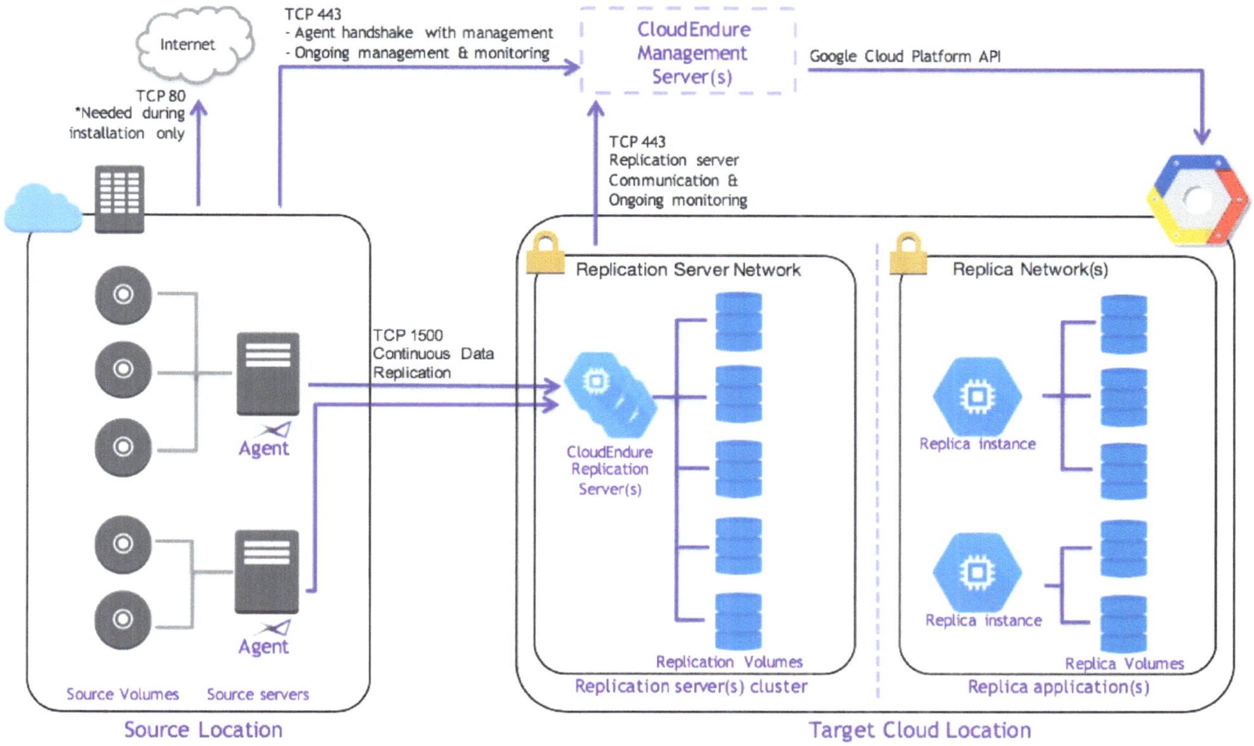

Figure 8 *Lift and Shift Migration*

For instance, Azure Migrate allows organizations to assess their VM environment, estimate the cost of running those VMs in Azure, and execute migrations with minimal downtime. AWS MGN also allows for incremental replication of live server volumes to lessen the impact during migration.

Migrating Physical Servers

Server type tend to be migrated with more complications in so doing due to the facts that are associated with certain requirement of hardware form and old systems. The physical-to-virtual (P2V) conversion is very common in helping to prepare workloads or to containerize them to a format that is easily consumed in the cloud platform. VMware HCX for instance assists with P2V conversion by virtualizing the workload and transferring it to the cloud securely.

In the case where the applications cannot be virtualized organizations have the option of containerizing the workload or using a hybrid cloud model where the organizational core applications stay on premise but can touch the cloud.

Migrating Unstructured Data

Documents, multimedia files, and logs, etc. constitute a large proportion of enterprise data and yet it is unstructured. Converting this type of data is a significant challenge to enable compatibility with cloud-based file systems and take minimum time for migrating data.

Azure File Sync, AWS DataSync and Google Transfer Appliance are created to migrate unstructured data at a large scale. These tools provide things like incremental sync – this just moves files that have modified from the last migration and therefore does not utilize network bandwidth. Azure File Sync for example allows organizations to store an on-premises cache of the most accessed files and the rest in the cloud. This hybrid model saves end-user latency.

Migrating Structured Data

Data placed in relational and NoSQL databases may be considered as the core of various enterprise-level applications. Transferring that data is a delicate process as the information is often considered vital to the company's missions.

Relational Databases

Currently, relational databases like Microsoft SQL server, MySQL, PostgreSQL etc., are very commonly supported by the cloud service providers. Others such as AWS DMS and Azure DMS tools come with built in functionalities of converting schema, and replicating and checking for data integrity as one migrates. These tools include the support for- Homogeneous migrations and Heterogeneous migrations such as Azure SQL database to SQL Server or Oracle to PostgreSQL.

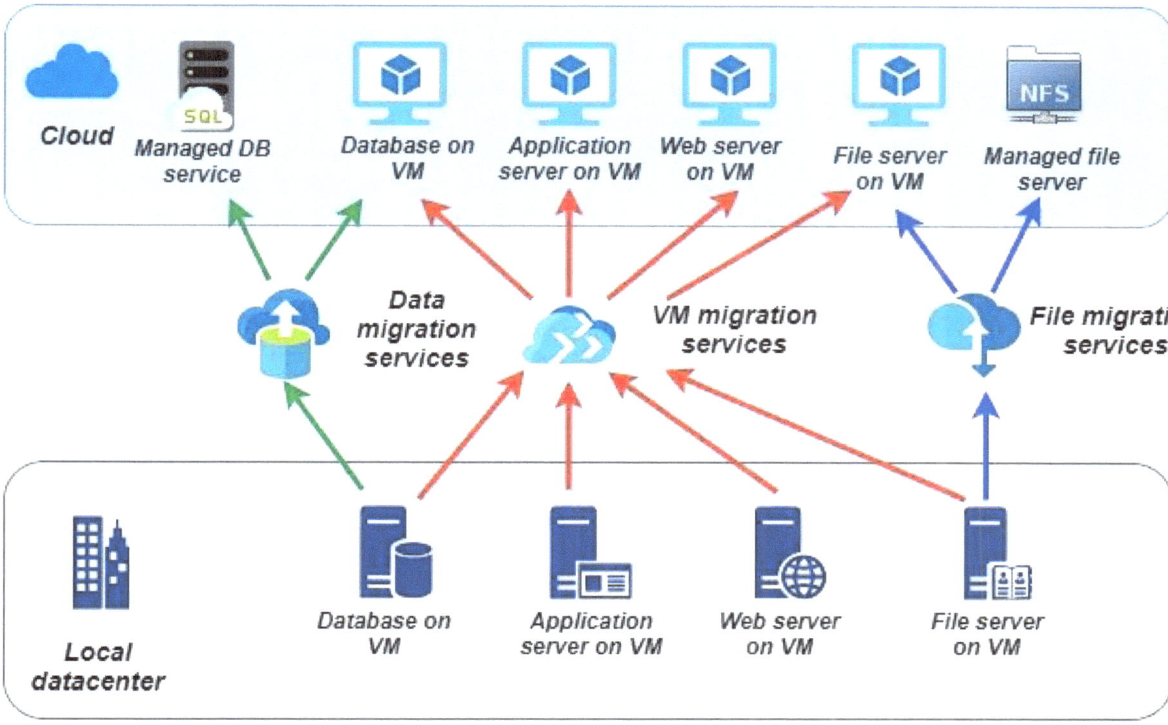

Figure 9 *Cloud Migration*

For instance, Azure Database Migration Service enables users to migrate SQL Server databases by allowing data replication continuously and in return helps minimize down time. AWS DMS is similarly loaded and can handle non-relational databases in addition to relational ones and therefore can be used for any type of workload.

Non-Relational Databases

For non-relational databases like MongoDB, Cassandra, and DynamoDB, the use of specific tools and services is indispensable. Transfer of large-scale distributed datasets can be easier with BigQuery Migration Service offered by Google Cloud and MongoDB Atlas Data Migration. These tools guarantee high availability during migration and supply optimal data partitioning and indexing schemes in the target environment.

An example of PowerShell script for architecture of migrating structured data from SQL Server database to Azure SQL Database is displayed below.

```
-- PowerShell Script for SQL Database Migration to Azure
Set-AzSqlDatabase -ResourceGroupName "MyResourceGroup" -ServerName "MySourceServer" `
                  -DatabaseName "MyDatabase" -TargetServerName "MyTargetServer" `
                  -TargetDatabaseName "TargetDatabase" -Edition "Standard" `
                  -ServiceObjectiveName "S2" -StorageMB 5120
```

Figure 10 Code Snippet for Azure SQL

Tools

The option of migration tools determines the effectiveness, dependability, and cost of migration. Each tool is tailored for specific workloads, so organizations should choose the appropriate tool based on the workload and business needs.

The following table 5 highlights the comparison of few of the most used migration tools.

Table 5 *Migration Tools*

Feature/Aspect	**Azure Migrate**	**AWS Application Migration Service**	**Google Transfer Appliance**	**VMware HCX**	**AWS DMS**
Cost	Free	Free	Hardware cost applies	Subscriptio n-based	Pay-as-you-go
Compatibility	VMware, Hyper-V VMs and Physical	VMware, Hyper-V VMs and Physical	On-premises data stores	Multi-cloud, hybrid	Relational/NoS QL databases
Incremental Sync	Yes	Yes	No	Yes	Yes
Ease of Use	User-friendly	Moderate	Simple for file transfers	Requires expertise	User-friendly
Scalability	High	High	Limited	High	High
Customization Options	Extensive	Basic	Minimal	Advanced	Moderate

Key Steps

1. Assess the current IT environment architecture, business and technical workloads, as well as data assets. Organizations must pre-define migration objectives and select tools based on those goals.
2. Perform a test migration to enhance the confirmation of such processes, detection of these risks, and to consecutively fine-tune these strategies to the business.
3. Mapping should be followed by data replication and transformation between the source and target environments, then intensive testing of the results.
4. Migrate applications softly in steps so as to minimize risks; first, start off with less critical applications.
5. To perform standard performance tests, identify and address performance problems, and lock down configurations for cloud security.

Change of the server and data requires skills, time, and the use of some tools to enable one to upgrade system. With different workloads including virtual machines, physical servers and structured and unstructured data, the migration requires a unique method to harmonize on the new model. With the use of such tools as Azure Migrate, AWS MGN, VMware HCX, organizations can reduce the time spent moving to cloud, reduce the cost, and also towards success in the long run.

Chapter 7: Deploying Workloads

Cloud computing has democratized the access and deployment of workloads in organizations and yet, the effective implementation relies on the principles of cloud excellence that guarantee efficiency, availability, and security. The Well-Architected Framework also referred to by the acronym WAF which was developed by cloud vendors such as AWS and Azure offers a guide for building workload that meets business objectives while effectively running operations.

This provides a theoretical guideline for assessing and optimizing workload architectures, which is based on the five fundamental factors that include the performance efficiency, reliability, security, cost optimization, and operational excellence.

Well-Architected Framework

The Well-Architected Framework is a set of guidelines that are intended to be used as a blueprint to ensure companies are doing the right things as they assess and optimize their workloads. Among its features, it provides best practices by workload, industry, and for different cases where workloads should be both scalable and strategically aligned with the organization.

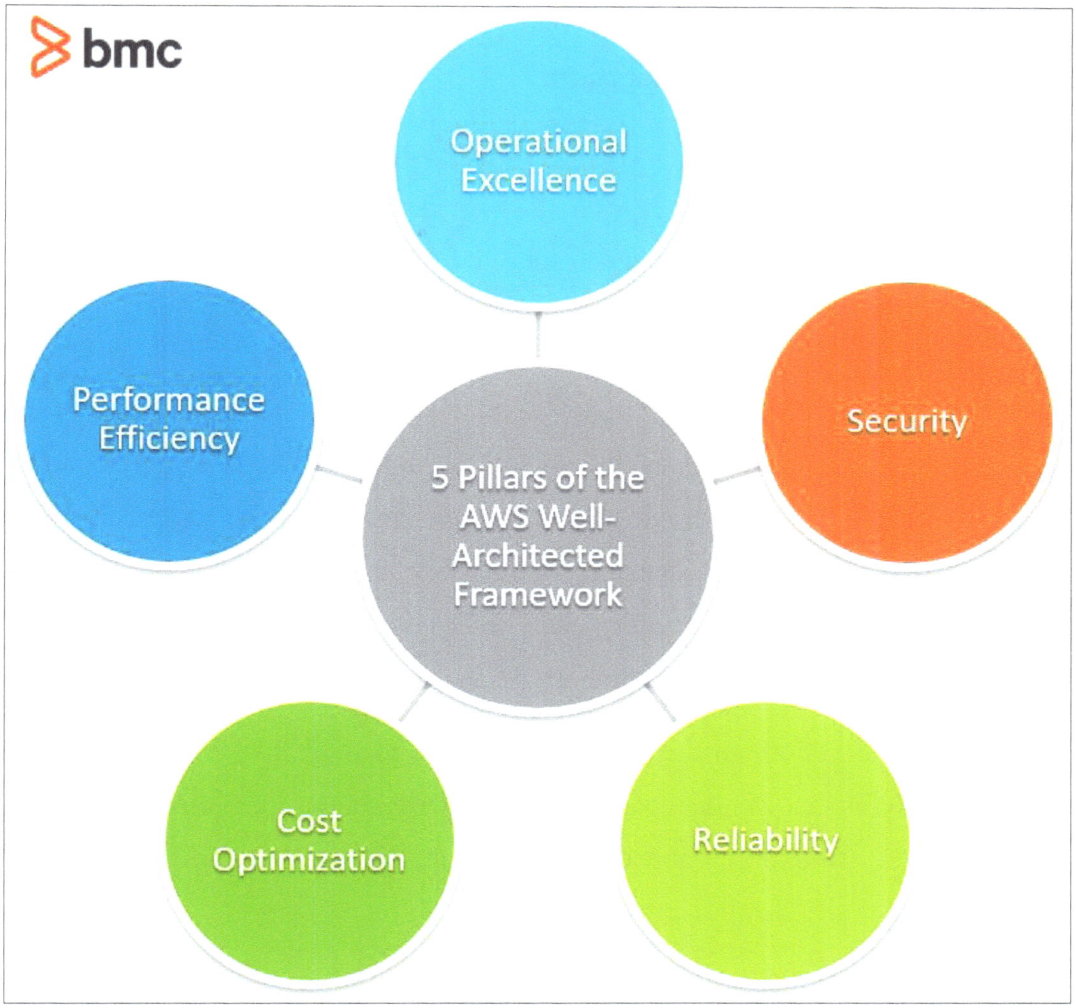

Figure 11 *Five pillars of WAF*

Each pillar of WAF focuses on specific aspects of workload architecture.

1. Performance Efficiency: This ensures that the workloads are efficiently utilized to meet demand and handle capacity fluctuations.

2. Reliability: Mainly considers the 'recovery rate' and achieves customer requirements for availability.

3. Security: Overviews ways of guarding our systems and data and/ or assets from unauthorized access, abuse or compromise in a manner that meets the legal or organizational requirements.

4. Cost Optimization: The objective of pursuing this strategy is to attain business goals needed for revenue generation in the least amount of resource use and expense.

5. Operational Excellence: Stresses on ongoing enhancement of processes connected to deployment, monitoring, and management.

Best Practices

Each pillar of the WAF offers the business a set of best practices to follow in order to achieve the end goal.

Performance Efficiency

Performance efficiency encompasses the identification of the right compute and storage infrastructure for workloads, leveraging serverless designs where it's practical, and keeping provisioned capacity adaptable to demand. For instance, running workloads with autoscaling policies helps systems manage the workloads according to traffic patterns and dynamically allocate or deallocate resources in an effort not to let the user endure high levels of latency.

To increase performance, organizational should employ methods like Amazon ElastiCache or Azure Cache for Redis, for caching data most recently used in the application. This slows down response time and increases the number of requests an application can handle per unit time where necessary.

Reliability

Reliability means system can work again if a workload fails and work can proceed in an expected manner. For example, running of workloads in a multiple geographical location increases availability since it insulates traffic from one area from unfortunate happenings in another location. Load balancers on cloud environments such as AWS Elastic Load Balancer (ELB) or Azure Traffic Manager are meant to be configured in a way that they can redirect traffic to healthy instances during a downtime.

A backup and disaster recovery solution are also important in this case. Weekly backup schedules and monthly DR testing should be integrated into organizational Workloads as a way of confirming its effectiveness.

Security

The security pillar deals with protection of workloads, and the kind of risks that may arise and the specific security standards, policies and measures to follow. These practices are IAM, encryption, and threat monitoring.

For instance, through AWS IAM or Azure Entra ID, it is possible to ensure that users, and applications, run with the lowest privileges necessary. Securing the transfers of information by emails with technologies like TLS, as well as securing data at rest using the AES-256 encryption.

Moreover, using applications such as AWS Security Hub or Azure Defender for Cloud to monitor the security of users, reveals anomalies and informs the administrators about problematic issues in real time.

Cost Optimization

Cost optimization involves maximizing the value of cloud investments by eliminating unnecessary spending and aligning expenses with the benefits received. This can be done through rightsizing; using spot instances for non-business critical applications; another through analysing usage patterns for any irregularities.

For instance, once an organization has subscribed to AWS Cost Explorer or Azure Cost Management, it can determine how much organizations are spending and act on any unused resources. The logical continuation of utilizing reserved instances for homogeneous processing of predictable workloads and serverless computing for event-based workloads also leads to cost optimizations without affecting overall throughput.

Archiving data that is accessed rarely helps you to reduce costs, as such data can be archived in AWS S3 Glacier or Azure Blob Storage Archive.

Operational Excellence

Operational excellence is interested in gradual enhancement of workload distribution, control, and management activities. The application of automation in an organizational setting has many benefits as can be seen from the following discussion. One of these is eliminating human errors in the variables while managing repetitive tasks

For instance, there is infrastructure as code tools such as the AWS CloudFormation and Azure Resource Manager template that ensure that infrastructures is deployed in the same format across the environments. Server's monitoring and logging solutions are AWS CloudWatch and Azure Monitor that reveal insights into system and user activity thus enabling early identification of and intervention on problems.

The other key practice is to set up CI/CD pipelines for application releasing to guarantee fast, consistent app updates. Tools such as AWS CodePipeline or Azure DevOps, makes it much easier to integrate and deliver into production changes fast enough to reflect the fast-changing needs of the business.

Steps

To apply workload deployment within Well-Architected Framework for optimization, the following steps are followed to ensure that architecture decisions align to the organization's objectives.

1. Establish a Well-Architected Review that will help to make an objective analysis of the company's strong and weak points as well as the possibilities to develop and grow.
2. Start by excluding the non-mission-critical jobs and functional areas and concentrate your optimization efforts on the reliable and secure program areas before you worry about lower costs or better performance.
3. Implement the recommendations formulated in the WAF pillars with regards to the highlighted deficits. For, example, to auto scale policies or implement IAM controls or optimize storage costs, for instance.
4. Engage tools and services from the cloud platforms in order to ease implementation. For example, Amazon Trusted Advisor provides performance, security, and cost optimization suggestions.
5. Proactively stress-test workloads and adapt architectures to align with evolving business demands or advancements in cloud technology. Check back occasionally with Well-Architected Reviews for compliance with the top recommendations.

The Well-Architected Framework serves as a robust and practical guide to design and run workloads with the desired outcomes and address the modern extensive set of requirements.

These five performance dimensions process efficiency, dependability, security, economy, and effectiveness support adaptive, secure, and scalable architectures that drive organizational performance

Whether this is the ability to scale out workloads on demand, governing access to data and information with IAM policies, or finding ways to reduce costs through reserved instance purchases, the WAF can simply be improved in one area and perfected in the other.

Chapter 8: Monitoring

With more and more workload being moved to the cloud, monitoring, backup and strong governance mechanisms are increasingly required to support organizational processes efficiency, data integrity and cost containment. These comprise the foundation of a stable cloud environment and the basis of which organizations may adapt to risks and secure their assets from threats while meeting regulations.

Monitoring

It is important to recognize that monitoring is one of the most basic processes in cloud because it offers organizations a direct view into the performance, resource usage patterns, and status of the systems and applications in the cloud environment. Through this tracking mechanism issues can easily be identified even before the user is affected, thus minimizing interruption to its users.

Cloud resources are scalable which means that resource can be scaled up or down as required. It can result in such undesirable effects as over-provisioning of resources and their under-utilization – all of which is reflected in performance and costs. Monitoring tools assist in tracking these fluctuations to support appropriate strategies aimed at fine-tuning such environments.

For example, the metrics relating to CPU, memory or networks usage as illustrated by tools like Azure Monitor and AWS CloudWatch are offered in form of a dashboard. It also can be configured to send notifications to the administrators when values exceeded certain limits, which helps make proper decision to solve possible problems.

A critical role in ensuring that application reliability is also exercised through monitoring. For instance, synthetic monitoring can perform sample transactions to identify transaction blockage, which may in turn, affect actual users; while log analysis which offers sheer understanding of the application usage patterns will assist developers trace and address problematic code.

Backup Strategies

Sometimes data loss can lead to severe consequences which would include operational down times, losses in reputation and even otherwise losses. Cloud backup strategies eliminate this risk for the simple reason that all important data must be backed up and can be restored in case of failure of any type, or if it has been erased on purpose or by accident, or in the case of ransomware attacks.

Principles of backing up as a service in the cloud includes the following.

1. Regular Backups: Set frequency of automatic backups to new times to minimize chances of undue loss of recent updates.
2. Redundancy: Back up the stores at different locations like different areas or regions, availability zones in order to be safe guard from failures that may occur at one area.
3. Versioning: Store several copies of data so that any incorrect data or data change resulting from an unauthorized person's actions can be reverted.
4. Testing: Backup and restore should be checked using test more often so that it can be known whether they are reliable or not.

Azure Backup and AWS Backup are the examples of solutions for policy-based, consistent protection of information in cloud workloads. These applications are compatible with other cloud solutions so that the backup process is organized from a single platform in compliance with retention policies. See Figure 12 for the flowchart.

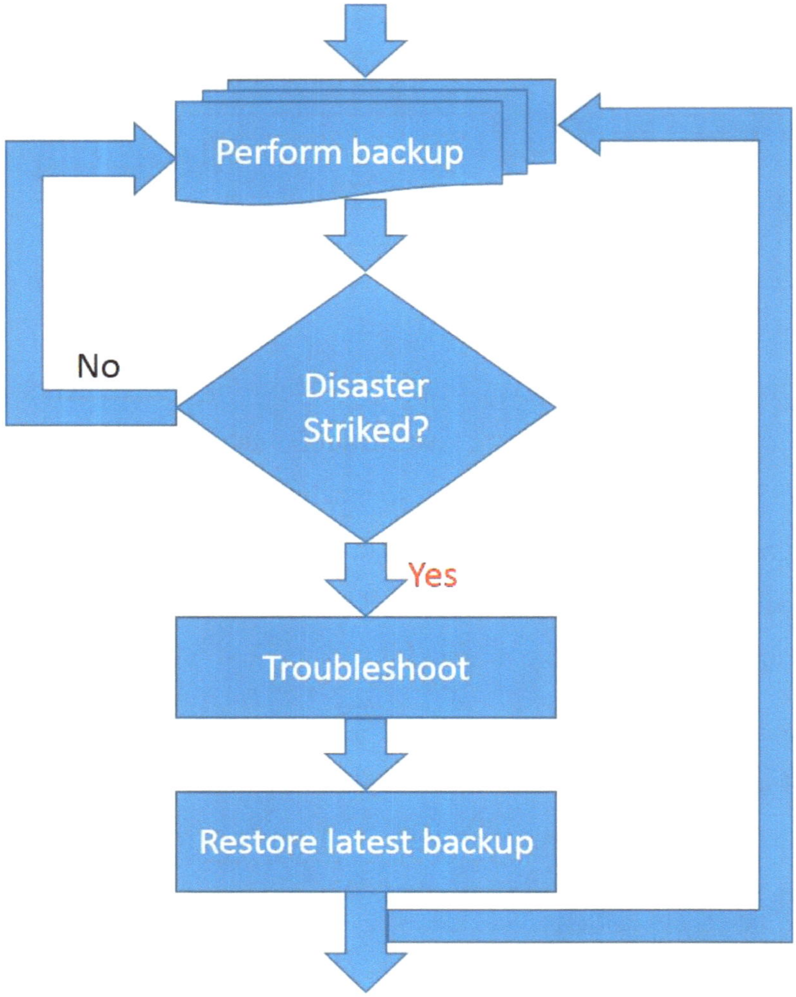

Figure 12 *Backup and Restore Flowchart*

Governance

Cloud management means policy and procedure to decide how the cloud resources need to be utilized in an optimal, secure and compliant manner. A strong governance activity is vital to mitigating some of these risks like outside access, high cost, and failure to meet the standard requirements.

Specific, real-life examples of key aspects of governance have been highlighted as follows:

1. Policy Management: To ensure we control the flow of resources used, factors like Azure Policy to set blocking policies on the use of resources ensures that it is standardized across all the teams and projects or AWS Organizations. For instance, policies can also restrict the use of non-compliant resources for example un-encrypted virtual machines.

2. Compliance Monitoring: Check compliance with Cloud standards on a regular basis starting with GDPR, HIPAA, or ISO 27001. Cloud-native tools including Azure Defender for Cloud and AWS Config enable users in discovering compliance issues, and mitigating them.

3. Cost Management: Minimize costs by creating constraints with the use of budgets, understand patterns of usage and expenditure. Making use of tools like Azure Cost Management services or AWS Budgets, consumers learn about their cost sources and guidelines on how to minimize misuse.

For instance, IAM is also facilitated by governance frameworks. By adoption such standards as least-privilege access and multi-factor authentication, organizations can reduce chances of compromise of its assets.

Tools

There are a lot of monitoring tools available in the market for use in organizations that adopt cloud environments and therefore, proper selection and implementation tools are mandatory the following general tools should be used preferably. Table 6 presents a concise comparison of the most widely recognized cloud monitoring tools, focusing on their features and compatibility.

Table 6 *Comparison of Tools*

Feature/Tool	Azure Monitor	AWS CloudWatch	Google Cloud Monitoring	Datadog	Prometheus
Metric Collection	✓	✓	✓	✓	✓
Log Analysis	✓	✓	✓	✓	
Custom Dashboards	✓	✓	✓	✓	✓
Alerting	✓	✓	✓	✓	✓
Cost Optimization	✓	✓			

Third-Party Integrations	✓	✓	✓	✓	
Open Source					✓
Multi-Cloud Support	Limited	Limited	Limited	✓	✓

The table above only give a brief overview of the capabilities of each tool which aid organization in choosing the most appropriate tool that meets their needs.

Monitoring and backup together with governance provide stability, security and achieve cloud optimality. Governance tools offer the insight that is required to achieve visibility over the performance of applications, and backup solutions guarantee that important data is not lost, and governance structures ensure that the policies to ensure compliance and costs are met are enforced.

For instance, the automated monitoring can detect variability in the usage patterns of the resources, and generate notification that enables the governances to decide on how to scale up or down the resources or change the policy. Likewise, backup also can be tracked for its success rate, and how well it adheres to retention policies, much to the requirement of governance.

Key practices for building a strong, secure, and financially resilient cloud include monitoring, backup, and governance. Cloud computing best practices also suggest the use of native cloud applications makes possible the implementation of higher-level policies, stronger security measures, and better overall detection and control of key information assets.

Adopting a positive attitude toward these elements not only minimizes risks and enhances the potential benefits of cloud for businesses but also allows them to fully capitalize on the opportunities cloud technology offers. From choosing an appropriate monitoring system to implementing backup measures and management controls, tactics ensure the development of a dependable cloud success system.

Chapter 9: Future Trends

The process of getting to the cloud is an innovative one not only for organizations, but also for the overall paradigm of technology as well. It represents a paradigm shift from traditional task-specific methods, which are slow, inflexible, and lack scalability, toward approaches that prioritize value addition, and the utilization of insights derived from data.

This makes it easier to practice several structured strategies, strong framework and implementing different standards of best practice. In this discussion, focus has been given to what constitutes the key framework for a successful migration strategy.

Starting from IT environment planning and its assessment to workload deployment and governance, each process lays down the cloud foundation. The tools and methodologies described: the Cloud Adoption Framework, the Well-Architected Framework, and the integration of monitoring and backup solutions emphasise that a successful and effective migration toward the cloud involves work that is systemic, interdisciplinary and ongoing.

Forums that would embark on this journey must not only concentrate on how it is done tactically but also on how the process is strategized to support the overall organizational goals. Laying the foundation to this argument, cloud migration is not only a technical process, but a strategic one. Companies are now not just integrating cloud technologies, but they are orchestrating their operations based on the opportunities the technologies provide them with.

The fact that cloud solutions can be easily scaled gives organizations a freedom to address issues like seasonal demand or expanding to new continents. Also, the cloud enables enterprises to harness new technological concepts such as artificial intelligence, machine learning, and big data in the petabyte scale besides revealing insights for competitiveness.

But this shift is not a piece of cake as it demands the new change of thinking in terms of legacy infrastructure, cutover of employees in terms of knowledge, and adjustment to serverless structures. In the coming years, the advances that will define the development of new technologies continue to occur in ways that are already changing the model of consumption and adoption of cloud computing.

For instance, hybrid cloud solutions are being embraced as organizations strive to adopt both public and private cloud, but with unique consideration to data sovereignty and latency issues.

This is because workload can be partially cast on the one environment and on the other, essentially leading to flexibility and reliability.

There is potential flexibility for companies that need a concentrated environment to meet high requirements of standards: private cloud deploying can be used after using public cloud services. This approach produces a win-win situation and empowers enterprises to achieve variety of aims without risking performance and security.

Another great disruptive movement is presented by edge computing that has emerged as one of the most influential vectors in the case of data handling. With the devices are getting smarter and connected, the Internet of Things (IoT) is still growing, there arises the need to perform more data processing at the edge.

This has been a challenge to decision making especially in the real time systems because of the long distance a data has to travel through the internet in order to reach a data center where computations are done. Edge computing in industries like healthcare, manufacturing and retail leads to instant response to event like alerts in patients monitoring, breakdown of equipment, or interacting with customers.

Edge computing is implemented alongside the cloud and thus make a continuous platform where the data can easily move between the edges of enterprise networks and centralized cloud solutions. One of the other emergent trends is the increase of multi-cloud usage where users apply several Cloud Service providers in order to achieve better costs, performance and service levels.

This approach reduces the vulnerability of lock-in effects that may occur when a business associates itself with vendors who offer a wide range of services while at the same time allowing a business to leverage on the distinct capabilities that different providers have to offer. For instance, an organisation may choose one cloud supplier for the AI computations but choose another cloud supplier for storage and databases. They also help with disaster recovery since data and applications can easily be spread across multiple locations in the different clouds, making it easier for an organization, to keep running in case of catastrophe.

The ever-rising interest in sustainability is also shaping the development of cloud computing as well. Green computing is fast becoming popular since IT providers are now paying attention to data center energy efficiency and the use of renewable power.

Today, organizations are calculating the environment footprint of IT and selecting the cloud partners that share the same views on sustainability. With the regulatory policies and customer demand for environmentally friendly solutions increasing continuously, it will not be surprising if the cloud industry also aims for increased sustainability.

While cloud computing is seen as a compelling technology, that has great future possibilities, businesses must also be wary of the risks that laying their bets on this technology brings. This is so because security is still paramount even as waves of cybercrimes continue to emerge. Security of data in a distributed environment mandates privacy, availability, and authentication or the use of security measures such as encryption and intrusion detection.

In addition, the move to the cloud requires more than technology solutions; there should be a change in organizational culture since most people in the organizations need to learn how to work with the new technology. Skills development and change initiatives are a critical starting point when sustaining innovation is an objective.

Cloud migration is not a one-off process but a continuous evolution of strategies and changes to try out in the cloud environment. Therefore, as organizations evolve, their approach to cloud adoption also changes. With the emergence of new challenges and requirements, fresh strategies must be developed.

This entails reflecting back on initial workings, considering the input of the other stakeholders and accepting review and change. Because cloud is a long-term strategy, the suggested projects focus shall be to keep the cloud infrastructure viable, appropriate for the enterprise, and delivering sustained value.

Finally, cloud migration stands as one of the greatest achievements of technological progress. It empowers companies to operate more efficiently, innovate like never before, and deliver higher levels of customer satisfaction. It goes beyond just tools; it's about transforming how companies operate and compete in a world increasingly shaped by the cloud. As such, cloud migration should be embraced as a crucial strategic move, with organizations leading the way in unlocking value and gaining a competitive edge as markets evolve

The contemporary environment of the cloud ecosystem requires organizations to understand newer trends and approaches to optimize the use of the technology. The combination of Hybrid cloud, edge computing, and multi-cloud strategies bring about interesting opportunities to enrich business value propositions.

Moreover, the raise of importance of sustainability and security indicates the need for ethical and reasonable use of new technologies. The process of cloud migration is one that is constantly changing and developing, which means organizations have to be constantly proactive.

With these strategies and perspectives in place, businesses can confidently move forward, transforming potential crises into opportunities that pave the way for a bright and innovative future. In doing so, they protect their position while simultaneously fostering the development

Glossary

1. Cloud Migration: The transfer of the workload and data storage in an organization from its physical infrastructure to cloud computing environment.

2. Cloud Adoption Framework (CAF): Best practice framework that offers a clear systematic guidance regarding how to approach cloud migration and management.

3. Landing Zone: A cloud solution specifically tailored to securely and optimally host application workloads immediately before, during, and after migration.

4. Well-Architected Framework (WAF): A list of recommendations for encountering workloads in the cloud that enhances reliability, security, performance, cost, and operation.

5. Edge Computing: Data computing approach where computations are done nearer to where the actual raw data is found for efficiency and real time results.

6. Hybrid Cloud: A hybrid computing model that interconnects the public and private cloud computing environments where flexibility and scalability are coupled with the need to meet security and compliance needs.

7. Multi-Cloud: The deployment of applications and services across multiple cloud environments to get the best of compute, storage and replication while avoiding issues associated with vendor lock-in.

8. IaaS (Infrastructure as a Service): A service provisioning model wherein consumers can obtain computing resources including server, storage and network on-demand.

9. PaaS (Platform as a Service): A deployment model where developers are given a cloud architecture and tools to construct their applications, perform testing and deploy them.

10. SaaS (Software as a Service): A model of cloud computing in which a company's software applications are centrally hosted and accessed by users over the Internet, on either a pay-as-you-go or pay-per-use basis.

11. Shared Responsibility Model: A model of how the security and management tasks are split between cloud service providers and users of services.

12. Azure Monitor: Microsoft Azure tool that mainly focuses on cloud monitoring and helps to analyze application and infrastructure utilization.

1. AWS CloudWatch: Amazon web service's cloud computing monitoring and tracking product to manage cloud resources, application monitoring and logging.
2. Terraform: An opensource Software defined infrastructure tool for provisioning data center environments based on code.
3. ARM Templates: Azure Resource Manager templates that previous used to define, as well as deploy, infrastructure resources in Azure environments.
4. Data Sovereignty: The idea that data that is digitally collected or stored is bound by the laws or regulations of the country in which it resides.
5. Backup Strategy: The process of pro-actively and methodically creating replica of data, for the main purpose of data recovery, in the event of data loss or alteration.
6. Governance: Measures that have been implemented in one or both of these contexts in order to regulate and/or minimize the risks of violation of compliance, security, and costs in cloud environments.
7. Azure Migrate: Microsoft's tool for planning and implementing migration of on-premise Windows servers, applications, and data to Windows Azure.
8. AWS Server Migration Service (SMS): An Amazon tool that aims at reducing the time taken to migrate servers to AWS cloud environment.
9. AWS Server Migration Service (SMS): One of the tools from the Amazon ecosystem that allowed for server migration to AWS cloud platforms.
10. Unstructured Data: Any files that are not in a set file organization format and can be in form of text, images or videos.
11. Structured Data: Structured information, which is easy to find, similar to a file in a folder or files in table format like in case of relation database.
12. Disaster Recovery: Systems, measures, and techniques employed to bring back lost IT services and data in case of a system either partial or total failure.

25. Encryption: A technique in data security where information is transformed electronically into a form that cannot be understood by any other person than the person who coded it.

1. Latency: This is where the ability of a network-based application's to operate is reduced because the transfer or processing of data within the network has been delayed.

2. Green Computing: Green computing procedures that can be applied in a computing environment, for instance, using energy efficient machines and power from renewable resources.

3. Sustainability: It is the ability to effectively manage an organization's technological systems in a manner that reduces resource wastage in the environment.

4. Compliance: Compliance that relates to legal, regulatory and organizational practices addressing matters of data and IT control.

5. PowerShell: A case of a task automation environment of a Microsoft's creation in the form of a command-line shell and scripting language.

6. CLI (Command Line Interface): A communicative interface that uses written text instructions to interact with software and other systems.

7. Cost Optimization: Methods used for the minimization of cloud costs while at the same time ensuring optimal performance.

8. Operational Excellence: The organisational strategy of making operations more specific and automated in order to improve their effectiveness and stability in cloud solutions.

9. Cloud-Native Architecture: A set of strategies for constructing software applications that are well-suited to the cloud deployment model in terms of microservices, containers, and serverless architectures.

10. Digital Transformation: That establishes and perpetuates the usage of digital technology to enhance business processes and therefore benefit customers.

www.ingramcontent.com/pod-product-compliance
Lightning Source LLC
Chambersburg PA
CBHW061316170726
48282CB00020B/108
9789366316666